Barnes continues across to go off Right, checks, changes his mind and quickly goes off the way he came as the houselights go up.

END OF ACT ONE

D1578903

ACT TWO

The living-room. Furniture has been crowded to
one side by the courtroom which dominates. Part
of one wall has had to go in order to make room
for it. Access to various parts of the room, and to
cupboards, involves squeezing with difficulty
round some part of the Court. Table, with two
chairs, is now downstage.
Even so, the Court is incomplete. There is a bench
for the Judge, a witness box to the Judge's left,
and benches for Counsel to his right.
Downstage Right is a small control panel for the
Court.
When the curtain rises MRS. GANTRY *is seen sitting at
the table.*
MRS. GROOMKIRBY *has almost finished pressing a
pair of black trousers. The jacket is hanging on a
hanger nearby.*

MRS. GANTRY: (*rising as at exit in Act One*). I think that's more
or less everything, Mabel.

MRS. G.: (*switching off the iron and hanging up the trousers
on the hanger with the jacket*). Finished, Myra?
I'll get your envelope.

MRS. GANTRY: I haven't touched the asparagus, but I can attend
to that first thing in the morning,

MRS. G.: (*she leaves the suit hanging from a peg*). Don't
worry about the asparagus, Myra. I can see to
that. It's those great packets of cereals they send
us. (*She finds the envelope.*) I think you'll find
that's right, Myra.

AUNT M.: (*off*). It's all the same, Mabel. Roller-skates,

53

	roundabouts, rickshaws. As long as it's getting us somewhere.
MRS. GANTRY:	You've had to move her, then.
MRS. G.:	(*indicating Court*). We can't get her in here for this great white elephant. (*To Aunt Mildred.*) You'd never be able to pull a rickshaw, Aunt Mildred. (*To Mrs. Gantry as they go out together.*) She wants something she can go over Niagara Falls in.
MRS. GANTRY:	(*at door*). She'd be better off with a barrel, Mabel.
MRS. G.:	(*following Mrs. Gantry out and closing the door*). Of course she would.
	Short pause.
	Sylvia enters from the hall in outdoor clothes.
SYLVIA:	Come on. I thought you were supposed to be ready.
	Stan appears from behind the control panel looking at his watch.
STAN:	You know we were going to be there by quarter to, don't you? It's now ten past.
SYLVIA:	Well come on then.
	Stan makes a final adjustment to something behind the panel and then switches it on as though to test it briefly for sound.
MRS. G.:	(*entering as Sylvia is about to go out*). This is a fine time to be going somewhere, I must say! (*She catches sight of Stan in passing on her way to the kitchen.*) The pair of you. (*She goes out.*)
SYLVIA:	(*at door. Impatiently*). Oh come on, for goodness' sake, and leave it.
JUDGE'S VOICE:	. . . and even your own counsel has to admit that not only were you as drunk as a wheelbarrow, but that you were quite incapable of so much as falling flat on your face when asked to do so. Moreover . . .
STAN:	(*switching off and following Sylvia out*). I wonder if he knows how much current this thing's going to eat up. (*Calling.*) Good night, Mrs. Groom-kirby. (*He goes out, closing the door behind him.*)

54

MRS. G.: (*entering with large tray*). Back goodness knows when, I suppose.

AUNT M: (*off*). Things seem to have been happening, Mabel.
Pause. Mrs. Groomkirby begins clearing everything from the table on to the tray.

AUNT M.: They've put me where I can see through the window. (*Pause.*) I think I must be in the station-master's office, Mabel. (*Pause.*) I can see out through the window. (*Pause.*) Did you know there were two Red Setters at the end of the garden, Mabel? (*Pause.*) I can see them from where I'm sitting.
Pause. Mrs. Groomkirby takes up the full tray and moves downstage with it on her way to the kitchen as Mr. Groomkirby enters from the hall.
He is wearing outdoor clothes and carries a large brown paper bag. He switches on the set from the control panel in passing, and puts the brown paper bag on a chair.

MRS. G.: A Mr. Justice called. (*Going off.*) Something about being on circuit.
Mr. Groomkirby takes off his hat and coat, opens the bag, and takes out a Judge's robe and wig. He begins trying these on, but they are too large for him.

MRS. G.: (*off*). To do with the mains, I expect. They've probably been looking at our electricity bills. (*Pause.*) What it's going to be like when it's *all* there eating up the current, goodness only knows! *The Judge materializes from out of the Court and advances upon Mr. Groomkirby who is at first unaware of him.*

AUNT M.: (*off*). Look at those two Red Setters, Mabel. I can see them from here at the end of the garden. (*Pause.*) They must be blue with cold out there, Mabel.

MRS. G.: (*off. Irritably*). Red Setters are *red*, Aunt Mildred!
The Judge now confronts Mr. Groomkirby.

JUDGE: Your wig? Or mine, Mr. Groomkirby?

55

Mr. Groomkirby, overawed, removes the wig.

MR. G.: Oh. Perhaps I've got hold of the wrong one. I thought . . .

JUDGE: It's an easy mistake to make, Mr. Groomkirby.

MR. G.: Yes—I'm sorry.

Mr. Groomkirby removes the robe and puts it on the Judge.

MR. G.: Rather silly of me. (*He adjusts the robe and fetches the wig.*) I thought it didn't seem quite right. (*He puts the wig on the Judge.*)

JUDGE: (*as he turns to go*). You'll in all probability be needed as a witness, Mr. Groomkirby. So be on hand. It saves wasting the time of the Court.

As the Judge disappears the Court begins gradually to assemble. A policeman, in uniform but without helmet, approaches Mr. Groomkirby with a sheet of paper.

POLICEMAN: Mr. Groomkirby?

MR. G.: Yes?

POLICEMAN: Through the door over there, please.

The Policeman looks round for someone else.

MR. G.: What's this for?

POLICEMAN: (*turning back to Mr. Groomkirby and jabbing with his finger toward the kitchen door*). Out there. With the other witnesses. (*Calling more respectfully.*) Detective-Sergeant Barnes?

Barnes appears downstage Left. Mr. Groomkirby goes resentfully out into the kitchen.

BARNES: Yes?

POLICEMAN: I think there's a strong possibility you may be wanted, sir, a bit later on.

BARNES: Right. (*Looking round the room.*) Been letting himself go a bit, hasn't he?

POLICEMAN: Beg your pardon, sir?

BARNES: (*with an offhand gesture towards the Court*). This lot. Plenty of it for a living-room.

POLICEMAN: Don't know where to stop, do they, some of them.

BARNES: (*going to door*). In here?

POLICEMAN: That's right, sir.
Barnes and Policeman go off.
The Court is now assembled and awaiting the Judge.
The Clerk calls for the Court to rise. The Judge
enters, bows to the Court, sits. Prosecuting Counsel
rises.

PROS. COUN.: M'lord. (*Addressing Jury.*) The facts you have
heard so far in this case, members of the jury,
have been simple enough and I do not propose . . .

JUDGE: (*intervening*). I see no sign of the jury. Are they
here?

PROS. COUN.: I understand they are, m'lord.

USHER: (*intervening*). There is no jury box, m'lord. As yet.

JUDGE: And no jury either apparently.

USHER: They are here in spirit, m'lord.

JUDGE: I see. (*He ponders momentarily.*) As long as they
are here in one form or another. (*He nods to*
Counsel.)

PROS. COUN.: The facts to which I am now going to direct your
attention, members of the jury, and upon which it
will be necessary for you to exercise your judgment
in due course, concern the activities of the accused
on a day last summer when he was allegedly . . .

JUDGE: (*intervening*). Where is the accused? Is he in the
court?

PROS. COUN.: He is in the dock, m'lord.

JUDGE: (*looking at it*). I see no dock.

USHER: The dock has not yet arrived, m'lord.

JUDGE: Where is it?

USHER: I understand it is on its way, m'lord.
Pause.

JUDGE: With the accused in it.

USHER: Yes, m'lord.
Defending Counsel rises.

DEF. COUN.: There have been certain delays, m'lord.

JUDGE: Traffic lights, I suppose.

DEF. COUN.: That and other untoward occurrences, m'lord.

JUDGE: He should be here. I have already disorganized

57

my personal arrangements pretty considerably in order to accommodate the court by being present, and I do not propose to put myself to further inconvenience by having this case running over time. If the accused is not here, the hearing will have to go on without him.

DEF. COUN.: As your lordship pleases.

Defending Counsel sits. Prosecuting Counsel rises.

PROS. COUN.: The whereabouts of the accused, members of the jury, on that vital day when he was allegedly elsewhere, tally in every single particular with the whereabouts of the only other person who so far as we know was on the spot at the time, and who is in the court at this moment. The whereabouts of this other person are therefore of paramount importance, and I should like to call him to the witness box now. (*To Usher.*) Mr. Groomkirby, please.

The Usher goes off.

Mrs. Groomkirby appears from the kitchen carrying a hot water bottle. She crosses to the door into the hall.

MRS. G.: I'm going up, Arthur. (*She opens door.*) You might notice what time Sylvia gets back. (*She goes out and closes door.*)

The Usher returns, approaches the Clerk and whispers to him. The Clerk stands and turns to enter into a whispered discussion with the Judge while the Usher withdraws respectfully.

JUDGE: (*looking across to Usher and addressing him*). Is this an objection to swearing per se?

USHER: Only to swearing on the unexpurgated Bible, m'lord. I understand there are certain passages he takes exception to, m'lord. On moral grounds.

JUDGE: (*after a pause for reflection*). Is he prepared to swear on anything?

USHER: I understand he has no objection to swearing on 'Uncle Tom's Cabin', m'lord.

JUDGE: On what?

58

USHER: 'Uncle Tom's Cabin', m'lord.

JUDGE: (*to Clerk*). I thought the issue of slavery on the American plantations had been settled by Abraham Lincoln?

CLERK: (*looking for confirmation to Usher*). I gather he has been informed of this, m'lord.

USHER: Yes, m'lord.

JUDGE: What did he say?

USHER: He said 'Not in my world it isn't'. Those were his words, m'lord.

JUDGE: (*to Clerk*). Which world is he referring to?

CLERK: I understand he has one of his own, m'lord.

JUDGE: Then why isn't he in it?

CLERK: He says he was told to come here, m'lord.
Pause. The Judge considers.

JUDGE: If it's a genuinely conscientious objection, I suppose I shall have to allow it. Has he got this work with him in Court?

USHER: He has a copy, yes, m'lord.

JUDGE: Tell him to bring it to the witness box.
The Usher goes out behind the Court. Counsel for the Defence rises.

DEF. COUN.: With very great respect, m'lord.

JUDGE: Yes?

DEF. COUN.: I have discussed this with my learned friend, m'lord, and if your lordship has no objection I should be most obliged if your lordship would consider dispensing with the oath altogether in respect of this witness, m'lord. I understand that if the oath is administered there is a strong possibility of prevarication, m'lord.

JUDGE: You mean he's a liar?

DEF. COUN.: Only when on oath, m'lord. I am told he looks on the oath in the light of a challenge, m'lord.

JUDGE: That's entirely a matter for him. If he's lying I shall direct the jury accordingly.

DEF. COUN.: As your lordship pleases.
Prosecuting Counsel rises. Defending Counsel sits.

PROS. COUN.: Might I, m'lord, with your lordship's permission, suggest to my learned friend that evidence from this source be accepted by the defence in the spirit in which it is given?

JUDGE: I suppose there's no objection. It would certainly save the time of the Court.

Prosecuting Counsel sits. Defending Counsel rises.

DEF. COUN.: Thank you, m'lord. My learned friend has suggested a way out of the difficulty and this is entirely acceptable to the defence, m'lord.

The Judge nods briefly.

The Usher enters followed by Mr. Groomkirby, whom he directs into the witness box. Mr. Groomkirby takes the oath.

MR. G.: (*holding up a copy of 'Uncle Tom's Cabin'*). I swear, by Harriet Beecher Stowe, that the evidence I shall give shall be the truth, the whole truth, and nothing but the truth.

JUDGE: You understand, do you, that you are now on oath?

MR. G.: I do, m'lord.

JUDGE: You understand what being on oath means?

MR. G.: Yes, m'lord.

JUDGE: It means that you have undertaken in the sight— in your case—of Harriet Beecher Stowe, to give honest answers, as honest and truthful as you can make them, in reply to questions which are shortly going to be put to you by learned counsel.

MR. G.: I understand that, m'lord.

JUDGE: Anything you are unsure about, or anything you have no direct knowledge of, you must not try to fill out in any way by the use of your imagination. You are here simply and solely to give the Court the facts as you know them. Anything more or less than this is not, and can never be, the truth. You must therefore in your answers avoid anything which is not to the best of your knowledge factually true. This is what the solemn undertaking you have given to the Court means.

60

MR. G.: I understand that, m'lord.

JUDGE: And you intend therefore to be bound by this undertaking?

MR. G.: No, m'lord.

JUDGE: You mean, in other words, that you intend to lie to the Court.

MR. G.: That is so, m'lord, yes.

JUDGE: A frank and honest reply.

Defending Counsel rises.

DEF. COUN.: With respect, m'lord.

JUDGE: Yes?

DEF. COUN.: This is a point for your lordship, but it would be of the greatest possible assistance to my friend and me, m'lord, and possibly to the jury later, if your lordship would give a ruling on this point of the witness's intended perjury at this stage, m'lord. The witness says he is lying, m'lord, but we have every reason to believe that in saying this he is lying.

JUDGE: And that he is, in fact, telling the truth?

DEF. COUN.: That is the dilemma we are in, m'lord.

JUDGE: No very great dilemma. This is clearly a witness of candid integrity upon whom it would be perfectly proper to place the utmost reliance.

DEF. COUN.: (*sitting*). As your lordship pleases.

Prosecuting Counsel rises.

PROS. COUN.: (*addressing Mr. Groomkirby*). Are you Arthur Rudge Groomkirby?

MR. G.: (*full of a confidence verging on truculence*). That's right, sir.

PROS. COUN.: And you live now—have been living since 1949— at 93 Chundragore Street.

MR. G.: Yes, sir. I had it done out back and front three years ago.

PROS. COUN.: By whom, Mr. Groomkirby?

MR. G.: By the deceased, sir.

JUDGE: (*intervening*). He was not, I take it, deceased at the time?

MR. G.: (*slightly patronizingly*). No, m'lord. He was alive when he did it.

PROS. COUN.: Mr. Groomkirby—I want you to cast your mind back a little way to the summer of last year. To the twenty-third of August. Do you happen to remember where you were, or what you were doing, on that day?

MR. G.: Yes, sir. I was in Chester-le-Street.

PROS. COUN.: What happened in Chester-le-Street on that day to cause you to remember it so clearly?

MR. G.: I interviewed someone there. About a life insurance.

PROS. COUN.: I take it you don't often go so far afield to interview people.

MR. G.: That's why I particularly remember it.

PROS. COUN.: I see. (*Pause.*) And this interview, you say, took place in Chester-le-Street on the twenty-third of August last year?

MR. G.: Yes, sir. It was a Tuesday.

PROS. COUN.: At what time on the Tuesday?

MR. G.: Three-fifteen, sir.

PROS. COUN.: At three-fifteen on Tuesday the twenty-third of August last year you were in Chester-le-Street interviewing this man about a life insurance policy.

JUDGE: (*testily*). He's already said he was.

PROS. COUN.: As your lordship pleases.

MR. G.: (*smugly*). It was a woman I interviewed. By the name of Myra Penelope Straightpiece Gantry.

PROS. COUN.: How certain are you, Mr. Groomkirby, of the exact time?

MR. G.: There was a clock striking the quarter just outside the window when I put my first question to her.

PROS. COUN.: And what was this first question, Mr. Groom-kirby?

MR. G.: I asked her if there was anything she would like to add, sir.

JUDGE: (*intervening*). What was her reply?

MR. G.: It was in the form of a sentence, m'lord.

JUDGE: We know it must have been in the form of a sentence, but what form did the sentence take?

MR. G.: (*feeling in his pocket and bringing out a notebook*). I made a note of it at the time, m'lord. (*Reads from notebook.*) She said she had a string of pearls in the form of a necklace but she wore it round her waist for the tightness.

PROS. COUN.: She wore it round her waist for the tightness. Didn't this strike you as being a rather extraordinary remark for her to make?

MR. G.: I didn't take much notice of it at the time, sir.

PROS. COUN.: You didn't think it at all remarkable. But you made a note of it.

MR. G.: (*smugly*). I was interviewing her, sir.

Pause.

Mr. Groomkirby has passed from semi-truculence to a sort of cocky assurance, but this is from now on broken down, at first by imperceptible degrees and then more and more rapidly.

PROS. COUN.: Would you agree, Mr. Groomkirby, that there were at the time possibly several thousand other inhabitants of Chester-le-Street equally eligible for interview, by you or someone else, on the subject of life insurance?

MR. G.: I dare say there would have been, yes, sir.

PROS. COUN.: But out of several thousand eligible people, the one person to be interviewed that afternoon happened, by a curious coincidence no doubt, to have been this woman, Myra Gantry?

MR. G.: If you put it like that, yes, I suppose that would be true.

PROS. COUN.: Even though the chances against it were several thousand to one?

MR. G.: I hadn't really thought of it in the light of a coincidence.

PROS. COUN.: Would you also agree, Mr. Groomkirby, that—confining ourselves to these islands alone—some-

63

thing of the order of fifty million people could, if the need had arisen, have gone to Chester-le-Street and interviewed this woman that afternoon?

MR. G.: I should think probably something of that order, yes, sir.

PROS. COUN.: The chances, in fact, were almost fifty million to one against its being you who did so?

MR. G.: I remember doing so, sir. I made a note of it at the time.

PROS. COUN.: Very well. And the time of this interview was three fifteen. A clock, you told us, was striking outside.

MR. G.: That's right, sir. I could hear it from where I was standing.

PROS. COUN.: And precisely at that very moment, when not one but both hands of the clock were at virtually the same point on the dial—at the figure three—precisely at the moment when the clock was striking the quarter, you put your first question to Myra Gantry.

MR. G.: (*defiantly*). Yes, sir.

PROS. COUN.: Perhaps you hadn't thought of that as a coincidence either, Mr. Groomkirby?

MR. G.: That was what happened, sir.

PROS. COUN.: You see, Mr. Groomkirby, this statement seems to be based upon a whole chain of these—to say the least of it—extraordinary coincidences. This question you put to Myra Gantry. You say it was your first. But in the course of an interview of this kind you might well have put twenty or thirty questions to her. This one, which happened—so we are asked to believe—to have been the first, could equally well it seems to me have been the seventh or the third or the twenty-ninth.

MR. G.: No, sir. It was the first.

PROS. COUN.: And this answer she is supposed to have given you. Goodness knows the words alone in the English language must be enough in all their

64

various forms virtually to defy computation—the possible ways of combining them must be infinite. And yet it was precisely *this* combination she hit on.

MR. G.: I made a note of it, sir.

PROS. COUN.: I know you did, Mr. Groomkirby. She said I have a string of pearls in the form of a necklace but I wear it round my waist for the tightness.

JUDGE: (*intervening*). For the what?

PROS. COUN.: For the tightness, m'lord.

MR. G.: That's what she said, sir.
Pause. Prosecuting Counsel sighs.

PROS. COUN.: Coincidence after coincidence. (*Lazily flicking through his papers.*) For instance you say all this took place on a Tuesday.

MR. G.: Tuesday the twenty-third of August, sir.

PROS. COUN.: You see, Mr. Groomkirby, I have here a calendar for last year and for a number of years prior to that. And I find that since 1950 there has been only one year in which the twenty-third of August has fallen on a Tuesday.

MR. G.: It fell on a Tuesday last year, sir.

PROS. COUN.: (*lazily delivering the coup de grâce*). The very year, in fact, when it so happened that Tuesday the twenty-third of August was the day you were in Chester-le-Street interviewing Myra Gantry.

MR. G.: (*dogged now, rather than cocky*). That's where I was, sir.
Long pause. Prosecuting Counsel flicks through his papers preparatory to changing course.

PROS. COUN.: (*in a quiet, bored voice*). There must have been quite a number of places from which you absented yourself on that rather vital twenty-third of August, Mr. Groomkirby, in order to be in Chester-le-Street?

MR. G.: I dare say that would be so, yes, sir.

PROS. COUN.: You were not, for instance, in London?

MR. G.: No, sir.

PROS. COUN.: Or Paris?

MR. G.: No, sir.

PROS. COUN.: Or Rome?

MR. G.: No, I wasn't there, sir.

PROS. COUN.: You were not, I imagine, in Reykjavik either?

MR. G.: I couldn't say for sure where that is, sir.

PROS. COUN.: Yet you absented yourself from it?

MR. G.: As far as I know, I did, yes.

PROS. COUN.: *And* from Kostroma.

MR. G.: I suppose I must have done.

PROS. COUN.: And Chengtu, and Farafangana, and Pocatello.

MR. G.: I'm afraid I'm not all that much good at geography.

PROS. COUN.: Not much good at geography, Mr. Groomkirby, yet you want the Court to believe that in order to be present at Chester-le-Street you absented yourself from a whole host of places which only an expert geographer could possibly be expected to have heard of.

MR. G.: (*beginning to flag*). That's where I thought I was, sir.

Pause.

PROS. COUN.: (*changing course again*). It is a good many months since all this happened, is it not, Mr. Groomkirby?

MR. G.: Several months, yes, sir.

PROS. COUN.: You have no doubt in your mind, all the same, that this person who interviewed Myra Gantry last August was the person I am addressing now?

MR. G.: It was me, sir.

PROS. COUN.: It was you. (*Pause.*) Mr. Groomkirby—do you know what happens to the body in sleep?

MR. G.: It recuperates its energies, sir.

PROS. COUN.: Certain chemical and other changes take place, do they not?

MR. G.: I understand they sometimes do, yes, sir.

PROS. COUN.: You must have spent a good many hours in sleep since last August?

MR. G.: I dare say that would be true, sir.

The Judge begins to look at Mr. Groomkirby with suspicion and curiosity from time to time.

PROS. COUN.: You must have eaten a good many meals, and absorbed a fair amount of food?

MR. G.: Yes, sir.

PROS. COUN.: It would be true to say, would it not, that the normal processes of what is known sometimes as metabolism, whereby body tissue is constantly being built up or broken down, have been going on unceasingly since the twenty-third of August last year?

MR. G.: I couldn't say, sir.

The Judge looks up and continues to stare intently at Mr. Groomkirby with the same curiosity and suspicion as before.

PROS. COUN.: I suggest to you, Mr. Groomkirby, that in view of these changes the man you say was in Chester-le-Street last year is not the man who is standing in the witness box at this moment.

JUDGE: (*intervening*). Are you suggesting he's someone else?

PROS. COUN.: It is the contention of the prosecution, m'lord, that he has been gradually replaced in the intervening period by the man who is now before the court.

JUDGE: (*to Mr. Groomkirby, accusingly*). Is this so?

MR. G.: It's difficult to say, sir.

JUDGE: Do you mean you're not *sure*?

MR. G.: Not to say sure, no, m'lord.

The Judge looks intently at Mr. Groomkirby for a moment longer and then nods to Counsel.

PROS. COUN.: Where were you, Mr. Groomkirby, before you came here today?

MR. G.: I was living in a world of my own, sir.

PROS. COUN.: Where, roughly, would this world be in relation to, say, Chester-le-Street?

MR. G.: Quite some way away.

PROS. COUN.: Your presence there, in other words, entailed travelling some distance.

MR. G.: Quite some distance, yes.

PROS. COUN.: Do you enjoy travelling, Mr. Groomkirby?

MR. G.: On the contrary, sir.

JUDGE: (*intervening*). You mean you actively dislike it?

MR. G.: Actively dislike it, m'lord.

PROS. COUN.: You actively dislike travelling and yet you made this lengthy journey to Chester-le-Street?

Mr. Groomkirby's answers are beginning to be made wildly at random in an attempt to satisfy the Court and so escape from it.

MR. G.: I was a masochist at the time, sir.

JUDGE: (*intervening*). A what?

PROS. COUN.: A masochist, m'lord. A term employed in certain quarters to denote an addiction to pain as a source of pleasure.

JUDGE: (*to Mr. Groomkirby*). Where does the pain come into it?

MR. G.: (*wildly*). I had myself tattooed on the way, m'lord.

JUDGE: Where?

MR. G.: On the train, m'lord, between Boreham Wood and . . .

JUDGE: Whereabouts on the body?

MR. G.: I had one done on my left arm, m'lord, and a Crown and Anchor on my right hip as we came into Watford.

JUDGE: Were there any others?

MR. G.: There was a butterfly design between my shoulder blades, m'lord.

JUDGE: Was this put on after the others?

MR. G.: Before, m'lord.

The Judge intensifies his look of suspicion.

MR. G.: In a tunnel outside Leeds.

JUDGE: How was it done?

MR. G.: (*relaxing momentarily on what seems safe ground*). It was done with a needle, m'lord.

JUDGE: We know it must have been done with a needle, but how well was it done?

MR. G.: (*nonplussed again*). Do you mean in my own opinion, m'lord?

JUDGE: In anyone's opinion!

MR. G.: I think it was up to standard, m'lord.

The Judge continues to stare for a moment at Mr. Groomkirby and then with the air of a man whose mind is made up nods to Counsel.

PROS. COUN.: You say you were a masochist, Mr. Groomkirby. Are you a masochist now?

MR. G.: (*fervently*). No, sir.

PROS. COUN.: When did you cease your masochism?

MR. G.: A month or two ago, sir.

PROS. COUN.: And what made you give it up?

MR. G.: It was taking up too much of my time.

JUDGE: (*intervening*). Too much of your time? And how long had you been a masochist when you suddenly decided that your time was so valuable that you could no longer spare any of it for your masochism?

MR. G.: For something like three or four years, m'lord.

PROS. COUN.: What was it that made you take it up in the first place?

MR. G.: I was at a loose end at the time, sir.

The Judge looks sharply up.

PROS. COUN.: You were at a loose end. Would you tell the court, Mr. Groomkirby, as clearly as you can in your own words, exactly how loose this end was?

MR. G.: It was worn right down, sir.

JUDGE: (*intervening*). Worn right down. That tells us very little. Was it swinging loose? Was it rattling about?

Counsel, with a barely perceptible sigh and the briefest of glances towards Counsel for the Defence, sits down.

MR. G.: It was practically hanging off, m'lord.

JUDGE: And this is the end you say you were *at*? This

loose end that in your own words was practically
hanging off?

MR. G.: I was pretty nearly at it, m'lord.

JUDGE: You told the Court a moment ago you were at it.
Now you say 'pretty nearly at it'. Which of these
assertions is the true one?

MR. G.: It was touch and go, sir.

JUDGE: What was?

MR. G.: Whether I fell off, sir.

JUDGE: And what prevented you?

MR. G.: It was that or take up masochism, m'lord.

JUDGE: I see. The facts are beginning to emerge. You
took up masochism when you began to realize that
unless you did so the end you were at might come
away and you with it. And you remained loyal to
your masochism just so long as it suited you.

PROS. COUN.: (rising). With very great respect, m'lord . . .

JUDGE: The moment it was no longer useful to you you
abandoned it without the slightest compunction. I
can find no possible shred of excuse for behaviour
of this kind.

DEF. COUN.: . . . if I might have your indulgence for a
moment, m'lord . . .

JUDGE: The law would be moribund if it were unable to
deal with a case such as this, and I should be
failing in my duty if I were to allow a man of the
kind you have shown yourself to be to go at large.

PROS. COUN.: The *accused* will be here at any moment, m'lord.
Pause. Prosecuting Counsel sits in despair.

JUDGE: You will be remanded in custody while arrangements are being made to have you sent back to
the world you have come from and claim to have
been living in, where your activities will be of no
concern to anyone but yourself.
*Fast fade out lingering for a moment on the Judge.
Pause.
Door into hall opens. The light outside in the hall
shows Mrs. Groomkirby in a dressing-gown, standing*

at the door she has half opened fumbling with the switch and then speaking into the darkened room.

MRS. G.: *Now* what have you done? Fused the lights, I suppose?

There is no reply. She puts her head round the door but, seeing nothing, withdraws it again.

MRS. G.: If you're going to stay down here waiting up for the dawn again, I'll put this light out.

Mrs. Groomkirby waits for a reply. None comes.

MRS. G.: (*Closing door*). And then for goodness' sake come up to bed.

Pause.

The Judge and Mr. Groomkirby become dimly visible downstage.

JUDGE: Well, Mr. Groomkirby. There's rather more here than meets the eye, don't you think?

Pause.

MR. G.: (*there is a defensive edge on his voice*). They've got the blinds down.

JUDGE: Possibly. (*Pause.*) At all events we shall know as soon as it's light enough to see anything.

Pause.

MR. G.: (*there is a surly edge on his defensiveness*). We're not going to see much with the blinds down.

Mr. Groomkirby becomes cowed, sullen, resentful, belligerent by turns.

JUDGE: You should have brought a torch, Mr. Groom-kirby.

Pause.

The Judge approaches the table, which is now downstage and has a chair on either side of it.

JUDGE: (*about to sit at the table where he can see Mr. Groomkirby*). In the meantime (*sitting*) perhaps it would be best if we were to play three-handed whist together.

MR. G.: Just the two of us?

Pause.

JUDGE: How many did you want, Mr. Groomkirby?

71

Mr. Groomkirby finds himself moving imperceptibly nearer to the Judge.

MR. G.: Three-handed whist isn't a game to play between two people.

JUDGE: I see. And why not, Mr. Groomkirby?
Pause.

MR. G.: *(moving still nearer).* And even if it were, we can't see to play.

JUDGE: Only because there isn't enough light, Mr. Groomkirby. Where are the cards?

MR. G.: I haven't got any cards.

JUDGE: You mean you've lost them?

MR. G.: I never had any.
Pause.

JUDGE: I think it might be as well, Mr. Groomkirby, if you were to go outside and look for some light.
Mr. Groomkirby is seen to hesitate for a moment. Then his resistance crumbles and he moves off.
Pause.
Mr. Groomkirby returns.
Pause.

JUDGE: Well?

MR. G.: Not a sound.
Pause.

JUDGE: Oh. *(Pause.)* And the light?
Pause.

JUDGE: What about the light?

MR. G.: I didn't see any.

JUDGE: Where did you look?

MR. G.: I had my eyes shut. *(Pause.)* I don't intend to be blinded suddenly by the sunrise.
Pause.

JUDGE: Or deafened, I suppose—by the dawn chorus. *(Pause.)* What precautions are you taking against that?
Pause.

MR. G.: *(reluctantly).* I wear earplugs.
Pause.

72

JUDGE: That perhaps is why you weren't able to hear anything out there, Mr. Groomkirby.

MR. G.: There was nothing to hear!
Pause.

JUDGE: You were wearing earplugs, Mr. Groomkirby.

MR. G.: It was silent out there, I tell you!

JUDGE: Faulty earplugs evidently.
Pause.

JUDGE: You could be as sure as you like about it as long as you knew your earplugs to be faulty.
Pause.

JUDGE: But not otherwise, Mr. Groomkirby.
Pause.

JUDGE: *Were* they faulty?
Pause.

JUDGE: I'm asking you a question! Were your earplugs faulty?

MR. G.: What if they were?

JUDGE: I see.
Pause.

MR. G.: What is it to you if I wear faulty earplugs?
Pause.

JUDGE: We'll play three-handed whist, shall we?
The Judge begins shuffling imaginary cards and then deals them on to the table.

MR. G.: (*slowly drawing nearer to the table*). Who's going to be dummy?

JUDGE: You, Mr. Groomkirby.
Pause.

MR. G.: (*sitting*). I've got my own hand to play.

JUDGE: You can leave that to me.
Pause.

MR. G.: (*picking up his cards*). It's too dark for this sort of thing.
Both go through the motions of playing whist.

MR. G.: If you play my hand, who's going to play yours?

JUDGE: I don't think we need either of us worry too much about that.

73

Pause. They continue to play in silence.

JUDGE: It's in some ways a pity you forgot to bring the cards, Mr. Groomkirby, but we seem to be managing quite well without them. My trick.
Pause. The game continues.

MR. G.: I feel cold.

JUDGE: You should have taken precautions.
Pause. The game continues.

JUDGE: My trick.

MR. G.: What possible precautions could I have taken?

JUDGE: You could have come here for one thing on a warmer night.

MR. G.: There aren't any warmer nights at this time of the year.

JUDGE: My trick.

MR. G.: You know that as well as I do.

JUDGE: (*gathering up the cards*). Go and see whether it's light yet outside. There's a good fellow.
Mr. Groomkirby hesitates, then gets up and goes out as before. He returns and sits down. Pause.

JUDGE: Well?

MR. G.: Frost.
Pause.

JUDGE: You were right then about its being cold, Mr. Groomkirby.

MR. G.: It's colder in here than it was outside.

JUDGE: You may well be right about that too, Mr. Groomkirby. But is it darker?
Pause.

JUDGE: I said is it darker in here than it was outside?

MR. G.: How the hell can I tell? You know I'm as blind as a bat with my eyes closed!
Pause.

JUDGE: Mr. Groomkirby. I wonder if you'd mind taking out your earplugs for a moment.
Mr. Groomkirby reluctantly takes them out.

JUDGE: Well?
Pause.

74

JUDGE: What do you notice?

Mr. Groomkirby makes signs with his hands.

JUDGE: Do you notice anything?

Mr. Groomkirby begins again making signs and then with a shrug abandons the attempt.

JUDGE: What's the matter with you?

Mr. Groomkirby sits motionless.

JUDGE: Cold, blind, deaf—and now dumb! (*Loudly.*) For God's sake, Mr. Groomkirby! Put your earplugs back in!

Mr. Groomkirby begins slowly replacing his earplugs.

JUDGE: Why do I shout? I dare say he can't hear a word without his crutches.

MR. G.: You think I'm paralysed, don't you?

JUDGE: I don't doubt you'll show us a clean enough pair of heels once your teeth have had proper attention.

Pause.

JUDGE: (*savagely*). Are you dentally fit?

Pause.

JUDGE: No. I thought not.

The lights come fully up. The courtroom is empty but for the three weighing machines of ACT ONE which stand, covered up, in the well of the Court.

MR. G.: (*with monumental relief*). Dawn!

JUDGE: (*rising*). Punctual as ever!

At the kitchen door is Sylvia. She is in her stockinged feet and carrying her shoes in her hand. The other hand is on the light switch as the lights go up, but she takes it away in order to signal to someone else out of sight in the kitchen. She retreats and closes the door.

The Judge looks at his watch as he rises, and then from his watch across to the death's head on the mantelpiece as though at a clock and compares the 'time'. He then goes up to the death's head, takes it up and shakes it as though starting a clock which has stopped. He puts it to his ear and, satisfied, replaces it.

75

He turns away and without a glance at Mr. Groom-
kirby goes into the courtroom and out of sight.
Mr. Groomkirby has the air of a man coming round
after a concussion. He has got up and made his way
in a dazed manner towards the courtroom.

MR. G.: God! What a night!

He goes, still dazed, to the Clerk's table, where he
absentmindedly gathers up some papers and wanders
off out of sight with them.
Sylvia tentatively opens the kitchen door.

SYLVIA: (*looking in. Good-humouredly.*) Don't be a fool,
Stan. He didn't say any such thing!

STAN: (*off*). Ask Tony. He was there.

SYLVIA: (*entering*). Come on. It's all clear.

STAN: (*off*). Right. Do you know there's some food out
here on a tray? And a flask?

SYLVIA: (*pirouetting round the room*). Bring it in then. (*As*
Stan enters with tray.) I don't believe he said any
such thing. What did *she* say?

STAN: (*putting the tray down*). I don't know. I didn't
stop to listen.

SYLVIA: We could do with some music.

STAN: There probably is some if you open the door.
(*Mimicking.*) Doh me soh doh soh.
They both take this up as a sort of comic duet, and
then, hotting it up, begin to jive to it.

STAN: (*as they approach the cash register*). Let's get the
Hallelujah Chorus. (*He clouts the cash register in*
passing.)

SYLVIA: (*breaking from him*). Don't be such a fool, Stan!
You'll have mum down here!
Stan goes to the door into the hall and opens it.

STAN: (*listening in mock consternation*). Not a sound.
Sylvia has crossed to the tray.

SYLVIA: You didn't bring any mustard in.

STAN: (*with exaggerated mock gallantry*). Good God!
(*Going posthaste into kitchen.*) How *could* I have
been so very careless!

76

Sylvia turns and looks into the mirror.

STAN: (*off*). Where the devil is it, anyway?

Sylvia has caught sight in the mirror of something behind her and transfixed with horror does not reply. Instead she spins round and faces the mantelpiece, gives a terrified look in the direction of her skull, and then turning away buries her face in her hands.

STAN: (*off*). It's all dried up, the only bit I can find out here. You'll have to do without by the look of it.

Sylvia has drawn her hands down her face and is looking out front with an expression of bewildered hopelessness.

Stan enters, sees Sylvia, and checks.

STAN: (*with a kind of dumbfounded solicitude*). What's the matter, Sylvia?

Sylvia looks straight ahead.

SYLVIA: (*flat voice*). Someone's been messing about with my death's head.

Stan looks across at the skull and back to Sylvia.

SYLVIA: (*turning and going out*). It wasn't working when you gave it to me.

Stan takes a step towards her, stops, watches her out of the room, and then turns to look at the skull. He stares at it for a time, then gazes down at the floor several feet in front of him and begins to turn away towards the kitchen door behind him. On an impulse, and mastering a strong reluctance, he goes instead up to the mantelpiece, takes up the skull, puts it straight into his pocket and turning on his heel goes out through the kitchen.

Pause.

Mr. Groomkirby emerges from the courtroom in a manner suggesting that he has been wandering around behind it all the time in a kind of trance, and with every sign of exhaustion makes his way slowly to the door into the hall.

When he reaches it he switches off the light in the room, which is now in total darkness.

As though at a signal the sound of Doh me soh doh soh comes from upstairs.

By the light in the hall Mr. Groomkirby can be seen to check, stiffen, listen, and then quite suddenly on an angry impulse turn back into the room, slam the door and so cut off the sound, and with a stride to the control panel violently switch on the Court.

MRS. G.: *(appearing at door)*. What's going on, Arthur? *The Court is assembled.*

USHER: Silence.

Prosecuting Counsel is on his feet addressing the Judge.

PROS. COUN.: The accused is Kirby Groomkirby.

MRS. G.: *(crossing to pick up suit)*. Oh, he'll need his suit then.

Mrs. Groomkirby crosses back with suit and goes out, taking Mr. Groomkirby with her.

Come on up, Arthur.

PROS. COUN.: M'lord, the facts, as your lordship is aware, are not in dispute in this case. The accused, Kirby Groomkirby, has admitted in the Magistrate's Court that between the first of August last year and the ninth of April he has been fairly regularly taking life, and since the case was heard there three weeks ago has asked for nine other offences in addition to the thirty-four in the original indictment to be taken into account, making a total altogether of forty-three. On the last occasion on which he took a life he was warned by Detective-Sergeant Barnes that complaints had been lodged and that action would be taken against him if he failed to conform to the law. It was after this, while he was preparing to repeat the offence, that Detective-Sergeant Barnes arrested him.

JUDGE: This would have been the forty-fourth offence?

PROS. COUN.: Yes, m'lord, but it was never carried out.

78

JUDGE: Because he was arrested.

PROS. COUN.: Yes, m'lord.

JUDGE: (*with heavy sarcasm*). It would be a pity to credit him with the wrong number of offences.

PROS. COUN.: He went before the Magistrate's Court on the third of this month where he pleaded guilty and was remanded for sentence. Since then he has asked for the nine other offences to be taken into account.

JUDGE: Are these nine offences exactly similar?

PROS. COUN.: They are exactly the same, m'lord, except that the victims are different.

JUDGE: Naturally the victims wouldn't be the same. What method has he been using?

PROS. COUN.: He seems to have been using the same technique fairly consistently, m'lord. He tells his victim a joke, waits for him to laugh, and then strikes him with an iron bar.

JUDGE: (*after pondering for a second*). Is there any previous record?

PROS. COUN.: No, m'lord.

JUDGE: He's been in no other kind of trouble at all?

PROS. COUN.: None at all, m'lord.

JUDGE: I see.

The Judge writes. Prosecuting Counsel sits.

JUDGE: (*to Defending Counsel*). Yes?

DEF. COUN.: (*rising*). M'lord, I should like to begin by calling Detective-Sergeant Barnes to the witness box.

Barnes is shown into the witness box by the Usher and sworn.

BARNES: I swear by Almighty God that the evidence I shall give shall be the truth, the whole truth, and nothing but the truth. Detective-Sergeant Barnes, Gamma Division.

DEF. COUN.: Sergeant Barnes, you I believe spoke to the accused and to his parents, shortly before he was arrested?

BARNES: That is so, yes, sir.

79

DEF. COUN.: Would it be true to say that you found him very communicative and helpful?

BARNES: He was as communicative as I understand he usually is, yes, sir.

DEF. COUN.: And helpful?

BARNES: He was quite helpful, yes, sir.

DEF. COUN.: Whom did you see first, Sergeant Barnes—the accused or his parents?

BARNES: I saw his parents to begin with, sir

DEF. COUN.: What did you say to them?

BARNES: I put the position to them, sir, and told them that complaints had been received about their son's conduct . . .

DEF. COUN.: Yes—I'm sorry to interrupt you, Sergeant Barnes, but perhaps you can tell the court what in so many words you said on this first occasion?

BARNES: Yes, I think I can remember what I said, sir. When I went in, the first person I saw was Mr. Groomkirby, so I addressed what I had to say to him. I said, to the best of my recollection, something to the effect that 'It's beginning to add up down at the mortuary, Mr. Groomkirby'.

JUDGE: (*intervening*). Meaning that you were keeping a check of this man's victims?

BARNES: We were rather pressed for space, m'lord.

JUDGE: I know that, Sergeant. What I'm asking you now is whether your remark 'It's beginning to add up down at the mortuary' referred to this man's victims only, or to those of other people as well.

BARNES: It was a kind of joke, m'lord. I was trying to keep on friendly terms at that stage and I made the remark in a somewhat humorous manner. I went on to say 'We haven't got the Albert Hall, Mr. Groomkirby'.

JUDGE: So you weren't giving information?

BARNES: Not what you might call information, no, m'lord. *The Judge returns the ball to Counsel.*

DEF. COUN.: What did Mr. Groomkirby say to you, as far as

80

you can remember, Sergeant Barnes, in reply to that remark of yours?

BARNES: It was Mrs. Groomkirby, sir. She said 'We shall have to have another word with him, Arthur'.

JUDGE: (*intervening*). Who is Arthur?

DEF. COUN.: The father, m'lord.

JUDGE: Arthur Groomkirby.

DEF. COUN.: Yes, m'lord. (*To Barnes*.) Did you get the impression from the conversation you had with the mother and father of the accused, Sergeant Barnes, that they were doing all they could to help their son and take his mind off law-breaking?

BARNES: I got the impression that they were very concerned at the turn things seemed to have been taking, sir.

DEF. COUN.: And genuinely determined to do what they could for their son, to get him to mend his ways?

BARNES: Yes, sir.

DEF. COUN.: And the accused—it would be true to say, wouldn't it, Sergeant Barnes, that he rather confided in you?

BARNES: He told me certain things about himself, yes, sir.

DEF. COUN.: Can you tell his lordship what you were able to gather from this conversation with the accused— and his parents—about his character in general, and what you think may have caused him to act as he did?

BARNES: He seemed to have a strong desire, m'lord, to wear black clothes. He told me he'd had it for as long as he could remember, and his mother, m'lord, told me the same. For the last year or two he's been studying what he calls logical analysis, and this has gradually taken the form of looking for a logical pretext for wearing his black clothes. Prior to that I understand he just wore them without concerning himself about finding a pretext, m'lord.

81

JUDGE: There's nothing reprehensible in his wanting to be rational about it.

BARNES: No, m'lord. But with the accused it seems to have combined rather adversely with this urge to wear black, m'lord.

JUDGE: In what way?

BARNES: He said he had to have rational grounds for wearing it, m'lord.

JUDGE: Yes?

BARNES: And he hit upon this idea of going into mourning.

JUDGE: For his own victims, I suppose.

BARNES: For his own victims, m'lord.

JUDGE: (after pondering for a second). Surely there must have been plenty of people dying from natural causes.

BARNES: He wouldn't wear mourning for anyone he didn't know, m'lord. I put that specifically to him. He said he felt it would be a mockery, m'lord.

JUDGE: Was he sincere about this?

BARNES: I think he was, m'lord, yes.

Judge nods imperceptibly to Counsel.

DEF. COUN.: I want you to look now, Sergeant, at the weighing machines there in front of the witness box. (*To Usher.*) Could we have Exhibit Nine uncovered, please.

The covers are removed from the weighing machines.

DEF. COUN.: Have you seen these machines, or machines like them, Sergeant, before?

BARNES: Yes, sir. I have.

DEF. COUN.: Where did you see them?

BARNES: They were upstairs with a good many more, sir, at the house where I interviewed the accused, sir.

DEF. COUN.: Are these the ordinary kind of weighing machines such as anyone going into an amusement arcade or into a chemist's shop might expect to find?

BARNES: They are a fairly common type, yes, sir.

DEF. COUN.: They are, in fact, what are sometimes known as Speak-your-weight machines?

82

BARNES: Yes, sir.

DEF. COUN.: How many of these machines did you find when you went to the house at which the accused was living?

BARNES: A good many, sir. I didn't count them, but I should say running into several hundred.

DEF. COUN.: Would the number you saw be consistent with there being five hundred of these machines?

BARNES: It would be consistent with that, yes, sir.

DEF. COUN.: Were you able to discover in your conversation with the accused, Sergeant Barnes, any motive he might possibly have for building up this exceptionally large collection of Speak-your-weight machines?

BARNES: He did refer to them, sir. I didn't set much store by what he said because I thought it sounded a bit far-fetched, but I gathered it was more the volume of sound he was concerned about. He wanted them to be heard over a long distance.

DEF. COUN.: By anyone in particular?

BARNES: By as many people as possible, sir.

DEF. COUN.: He was teaching them to sing, wasn't he, Sergeant?

BARNES: That was his intention, sir.

JUDGE: To do *what*?

DEF. COUN.: To sing, m'lord.

JUDGE: I thought we were talking about weighing machines?

DEF. COUN.: These are a special type, m'lord, which speak when subjected to weight and can also be trained to sing. I have had these three brought into the Court for this reason, m'lord. There would be no difficulty in arranging for them to sing a short song, or part of a song, if your lordship would allow.

JUDGE: How long is this going to take?

DEF. COUN.: It would take a matter of minutes, m'lord.

JUDGE: (*unenthusiastically*). Yes. I suppose so.

DEF. COUN.: I am very much obliged to your lordship.
Defending Counsel nods to Usher.
The Usher lifts a weight on to each of the three weighing machines in turn.
When all three weights have been placed in position, the Usher gives middle C on a whistle.
After a brief pause Numbers Two and Three launch into the Lizzie Borden song as a duet. Number One is silent.
The Judge, in so far as he takes notice of the song at all, remains unimpressed by it.
The song ends.
Pause.

DEF. COUN.: (*rising*). Thank you, m'lord.
The Usher removes the weight first from Two and then from Three.

DEF. COUN.: (*as Usher goes to remove the weight from Number One*). One final question, Sergeant Barnes.

NUMBER ONE: (*as weight is removed*). Fifteen stone ten pounds.
There is a pause for one puzzled moment.

DEF. COUN.: (*resuming*). Was anything said to you, Sergeant Barnes, either by the accused or by his parents, that might lead you to believe he was intending eventually to have these weighing machines shipped to the North Pole?

BARNES: Yes, sir. Arrangements were actually in hand for this, sir.

DEF. COUN.: Did he volunteer any information that might explain this action?

BARNES: Only to say that he wanted them to act as sirens, sir.

JUDGE: (*intervening*). Sirens?

BARNES: (*in an explanatory manner*). To lure people to the North Pole, m'lord.

DEF. COUN.: There was a scientific reason for this, Sergeant Barnes, wasn't there?

BARNES: Yes, sir.

DEF. COUN.: Will you try and enlarge on this for his lordship, Sergeant Barnes?

84

BARNES: (*to Judge*). I fancy he had some notion, m'lord, that once these people were at the North Pole, if he could get enough of them together in the one place, he would have very little difficulty in persuading them all to jump at the same moment.

JUDGE: And what inscrutable purpose was this manoeuvre calculated to serve?

BARNES: I think he was more concerned with what would happen when they landed again, m'lord. He was hoping it might have the effect of tilting the earth's axis a little more to one side, m'lord. *Pause.*

JUDGE: I see.

DEF. COUN.: This would very likely bring about quite far-reaching climatic changes, would it not, Sergeant?

BARNES: I think something of that kind was what he had in mind, sir.

DEF. COUN.: A shifting of the Ice Cap, for instance.

BARNES: Yes, sir.

DEF. COUN.: This might well give rise to a new Ice Age so far as these islands are concerned?

BARNES: In all probability, yes, sir.

DEF. COUN.: Would it be true to say, Sergeant Barnes, that he was hoping in this way to provide himself with a self-perpetuating pretext for wearing black?

BARNES: Yes, sir.

DEF. COUN.: By ensuring that for an indefinite period deaths from various causes connected with the excessive cold would be many and frequent?

BARNES: That was at the back of it, yes, sir.

DEF. COUN.: Thank you, Sergeant Barnes. *Barnes stands down.*

DEF. COUN.: I would like to call Mrs. Groomkirby now to the witness box. (*To Usher.*) Mrs. Groomkirby?

USHER: Mrs. Groomkirby!

POLICEMAN: Mrs. Groomkirby!

MRS. G.: (*off*). Give me time to get downstairs. (*Appearing from hall.*) Where do I go?

85

She is shown into the witness box.

MRS. G.: You feel so public.

In the witness box Mrs. Groomkirby becomes somewhat overawed by her surroundings.

She takes the oath.

DEF. COUN.: You are Mabel Laurentina Groomkirby.

MRS. G.: Yes, sir.

DEF. COUN.: You are the mother of the accused, Mrs. Groomkirby are you not?

MRS. G.: Oh. Well, yes. I suppose if he's on trial I must be. I hadn't realized.

DEF. COUN.: It would be true to say, wouldn't it, Mrs. Groomkirby, that your son likes wearing black?

MRS. G.: He's worn it all his life.

DEF. COUN.: He likes wearing black but he doesn't feel justified in wearing it except at the funeral of someone he knows?

MRS. G.: Well, it's only in the last few years he's come to think like that, really. He always used to just wear it.

DEF. COUN.: His attitude has changed?

MRS. G.: It's been very noticeable over the last year or two.

DEF. COUN.: Can you account for this change in any way, Mrs. Groomkirby?

MRS. G.: Not really—unless his studies have had anything to do with it. He's always been of a very logical turn of mind ever since he was born, but what with all this studying lately he seems to have got a different attitude altogether these last few years.

DEF. COUN.: Your son is a rather ingenious young man, is he not, Mrs. Groomkirby?

MRS. G.: A lot of people say he is, yes, sir.

DEF. COUN.: He has a cash register, I believe.

MRS. G.: That's right.

DEF. COUN.: What exactly is the function of this cash register, Mrs. Groomkirby? What does your son use it for?

MRS. G.: It was an egg-timer to begin with, and then he

gradually came to rely on it more and more for other things.

DEF. COUN.: When it was an egg-timer—can you tell his lordship how it worked?

MRS. G.: Well, sir, it was rigged up in the kitchen with the telephone on one side of it and the gas stove on the other. He likes to have his eggs done the exact time—just the four minutes ten seconds—or he won't eat them. He just goes right inside himself. So he rigged up the cash register.

DEF. COUN.: How did it work, Mrs. Groomkirby?

MRS. G.: He'd got a stop-watch but he wouldn't trust that. He'd trust it for the minutes but he wouldn't trust it for the seconds.

DEF. COUN.: And so he used the cash register instead?

MRS. G.: That and the telephone. He had them side by side.

DEF. COUN.: What was the actual procedure he adopted, Mrs. Groomkirby?

MRS. G.: Well, he'd put his egg on to boil, then he'd stand there with his stop-watch.

DEF. COUN.: Go on, Mrs. Groomkirby.

MRS. G.: Well, then the moment it said four minutes exactly on his stop-watch, he'd simply dial TIM, wait for the pips, ring up No Sale on the cash register and take out his egg.

DEF. COUN.: And this was, in fact, the only sequence of actions that took precisely the ten seconds?

MRS. G.: That's right, sir. He wouldn't eat them otherwise.

DEF. COUN.: And he worked this out for himself without any assistance whatever from anyone else?

MRS. G.: Oh, yes. It was entirely his own. And then he started getting dependent on the bell for other things as well. Eating first; and now practically everything he does he has to have a bell rung.

DEF. COUN.: To come back to this question of the black clothes, Mrs. Groomkirby.

MRS. G.: They've as good as told him that if ever he were

87

to part with his cash register it would mean total paralysis for him.

DEF. COUN.: Yes. You say your son, Mrs. Groomkirby, has always liked wearing black. Will you tell his lordship in your own words about this attachment to black clothes?

MRS. G.: Well, sir, all his baby things were black. He had a black shawl and rompers and even down to his bib were all black, and his sheets and pillow-cases. We had everything in black for him as soon as he was born. People used to stop in the street and remark about him. He's never worn anything white. Sometimes when he was in his pram people used to say he looked like a wee undertaker lying there. We got it all planned before he was born that if we had a white baby we were going to dress him in black—or her in black if it had been a girl—and if either of them were black we'd have everything white, so as to make a contrast. But when he came he was white so we had the black.

JUDGE: (intervening). Is your husband a coloured man, Mrs. Groomkirby?

MRS. G.: He's an insurance agent, sir.

JUDGE: Yes, but is he coloured?

MRS. G.: Well, no, sir. Not so far as I know.

JUDGE: What I'm trying to get from you, Mrs. Groomkirby, is the simple fact of your husband's racial characteristics. Does he, for instance, have any negro blood?

MRS. G.: Well—he *has* got one or two bottles up in his room, but he doesn't tell me what's *in* them. *The Judge looks blankly at Mrs. Groomkirby for a moment and then relinquishes the matter.*

DEF. COUN.: There's one more thing I should like to ask you, Mrs. Groomkirby. Each of your son's forty-three victims was struck with an iron bar after having been told a joke. Would it be true to say that your son, Mrs. Groomkirby, went to considerable trouble over these jokes?

MRS. G.: He went to very great trouble indeed, sir. He sat up to all hours thinking out jokes for them.

DEF. COUN.: Can you tell his lordship why your son went to all this trouble with every one of his forty-three victims, when there were a number of far simpler methods he could have used?

MRS. G.: I think for one thing he rather took to the humorous side of it. And for another thing he always wanted to do everything he could for these people. He felt very sorry for them.

DEF. COUN.: He wanted to make things as pleasant as possible for them even at some considerable trouble and inconvenience to himself?

MRS. G.: He didn't mind how much trouble he went to, as long as they ended on a gay note.

DEF. COUN.: Thank you, Mrs. Groomkirby.

Mrs. Groomkirby is invited by a sign from the Usher to stand down and does so with respectful restraint.

Once out of the aura of the Court, and in her own home, she resumes a brisker manner and picking up the tray goes into the kitchen with it.

Counsel for the Defence begins his speech to the Judge.

DEF. COUN.: M'lord, in asking you to take a lenient view of this case, I am not underestimating the seriousness of the offences this young man has committed. They are very grave breaches of the law, and no one realizes this now more than he does himself. He has made very considerable efforts to find other ways of satisfying this—in itself quite harmless, indeed laudable—desire for a logical pretext, but so far, unfortunately, he has met with little success. He has had this scheme involving the weighing machines. We may think this to have been a somewhat grandiose scheme and that there

89

could be very little hope of its succeeding, or even indeed of its being universally acceptable were it possible to adopt it; the important thing is that it has been worked out by this astonishingly resourceful and gifted young man as the result of a determination to avoid by every means in his power any further breach of the law in satisfying this craving he has for black clothes. He has gone to very great trouble and expense in training these weighing machines, m'lord, with the intention not of sitting idly down beside them to listen to and enjoy the fruits of his labours himself, but of keeping himself indirectly from coming into conflict with the law. In my respectful submission, m'lord, this very complex personality with whom we are dealing is not in any ordinary sense of the word a killer; he is, on the contrary, a kindly, rather gentle young man, not given to violence—except in this one respect—and showing himself to be quite exceptionally considerate of others even to the extent of arranging, at considerable personal sacrifice of time and energy, for them to die laughing. I would therefore ask your lordship to pass as light a sentence as, in your lordship's judgment, is warranted in this very exceptional case.

Defending Counsel sits.

Kirby appears, looking for Gormless. He checks on seeing Gormless and raises his baton.

The Judge addresses the accused.

Kirby drops to his knees facing the Judge.

JUDGE: There have been too many crimes of this nature: people killing a number of victims—forty-three in your case—from what appear to be, and indeed often are in themselves, laudable motives. Your counsel has made an eloquent plea for you, and two people have been willing to come into the witness box—one of them the detective who

arrested you—and give a favourable account of
you. But from your forty-three victims—not a
word. Not one of those forty-three has felt under
any obligation to come forward and speak for
you, notwithstanding the great trouble we are
told you went to in furnishing them with laughing
matter. And what about the iron bar you used?
Was this also chosen and wielded with the well-
being of your victims in mind? I think not. Your
mother has said that you wear black. This is not
surprising. Such a taste seems to me to be in
perfect conformity with the career you have
chosen to embark upon. I am not greatly influenced by the reasons that have been put
forward for your having this apparently irresistible
craving—they seem to me to have very little
bearing on the matter. It is becoming more and
more an accepted feature of cases of this kind that
in the course of them the court is subjected to a
farrago of psychological poppycock in which every
imaginable ailment in the nursery is prayed in aid.
As for your desire to find a logical pretext, this is
the one redeeming feature I have been able to
find in this case. But you could have come by a
pretext in any one of a number of quite legitimate
ways. I have no doubt at all that at least a score
of undertakers could have been found whose
advice and assistance you could have had for the
asking. Instead you chose another way, a way
which has led you straight to this court. You
began a few months ago by telling your first joke
to your first victim and then striking him with an
iron bar. What did you get out of it? The excuse
to wear black for a day or two. Was it really worth
breaking the law in order to be able to wear black
for forty-eight hours? And then a little later on
came your second murder, and the opportunity to
wear black again for a short time. And so it has

gone on: victim after victim, until even you could not have expected the authorities to overlook it any longer. Indeed Detective-Sergeant Barnes warned you quite explicitly what would happen if you broke the law for the forty-fourth time. There seems to me to be not the smallest shred of excuse for these repeated offences. As for this diabolical scheme to send weighing machines to the North Pole, which we have been told is so ingenious, the less said about it the better. If the song we have just had to listen to in this court is in any way typical of the kind of thing we were to have been regaled by from the North Pole, it would be hard to imagine what sort of person would have been enticed there by it—or having got there would want to remain for long within earshot, still less be in any fit state to jump up and down. In deciding upon the sentence I shall impose in this case, I have been influenced by one consideration, and it is this: that in sentencing a man for one crime, we may be putting him beyond the reach of the law in respect of those other crimes of which he might otherwise have become guilty. The law, however, is not to be cheated in this way. I shall therefore discharge you.

Mrs. Groomkirby enters from the hall on the last words of the Judge and rings up No Sale on the cash register.

This is the signal for a massed choir to launch into the Hallelujah Chorus, and for blackout of the Court and living-room.

Kirby flings out his arms to conduct choir.

Each alternate Hallelujah is sung by Gormless who is now lit up with the words 'I speak your weight' in red.

Gormless takes over from the massed choir, Kirby in a mood of ungainly gaiety conducts him, and finally, when Gormless relapses into silence takes out a

weight and crossing the forestage with it conducts
and accompanies its tiny piping treble in a gay
childlike rendering of the same Hallelujah Chorus.
He goes off Left.
The light comes up on the living-room.
The Court is empty. Mrs. Groomkirby is dusting it.
Sylvia is sitting as at the beginning of ACT ONE
in silence.

MRS. G.: (*with a nod towards the music stand which remains
where Kirby placed it*). What's that doing down
here?
Pause.

MRS. G.: You might take it up, Sylvia.

SYLVIA: (*looking up*). Take what up?

MRS. G.: (*going out to kitchen*). That thing whatever it is of
Kirby's. It's no business being down here.

SYLVIA: Can't he come and get it himself?

MRS. G.: (*off*). You know very well he's busy up there,
Sylvia.
*Sylvia shrugs, goes on reading for a moment, then
puts her magazine down and saunters out with the
music stand.*
*Barnes appears from the forestage Left. He is getting
into his overcoat and calls somewhat defensively to
Mrs. Groomkirby.*

BARNES: Thank you, Mrs. Groomkirby.
*Mrs. Groomkirby enters from the kitchen with a tray
of food which she sets out on the table as for Mrs.
Gantry.*

MRS. G.: Just off, are you?

BARNES: Yes—they've had a good look round and . . .
Sylvia enters from the hall and sits with magazine.

MRS. G.: (*without looking up from her work*). Seen all they
want, have they?

BARNES: I think they have, yes. More or less. (*Edging off.*)

MRS. G.: (*half to herself*). Day in day out. Gawping. The
place isn't your own.

BARNES: (*escaping*). Back tomorrow about half past seven

93

then, Mrs. Groomkirby—if that's all right.

MRS. G.: They won't have to come expecting anything.

BARNES: I'll tell them. Good-bye, Mrs. Groomkirby. Good-bye, Sylvia. (*Barnes goes off.*)
Mr. Groomkirby enters from the hall and crosses the stage slowly with a book open in his hand. He has on the Judge's wig and robe. Neither seems to be made for him.

SYLVIA: (*without looking up*). I don't know why they don't all go and stand outside Buckingham Palace or something instead.

MR. G.: (*trying out what he thinks may be an appropriate voice and manner as he reads. At large*). That, members of the jury, is the evidence before you.
Dissatisfied, he moves further right and takes up one or two tentative stances.

SYLVIA: Or the Taj Mahal or something. And gawp at that, instead.

MR. G.: (*in an undertone*). That, members of the jury . . .
He abandons it and tries again.

AUNT M.: On roller-skates. By moonlight. To Outer Space!

MR. G.: (*he has got it right and addresses Gormless without recognition as though speaking to the Foreman of the jury*). That, members of the jury, is the evidence before you. (*He turns to go, delivering his final words in a dismissively offhand manner.*) What weight you give to it is a matter entirely for you.

GORMLESS: (*lighting up*). Fifteen stone ten pounds.
The sound stops Mr. Groomkirby in his tracks. He turns, startled, puzzled, deflated in turn. He goes hopelessly off.

CURTAIN